W9-BED-164

Property of)
FAMILY OF FAITH
LIBRARY

HOW TO REACH GROUP DECISIONS

Family of Faith Library

HOW TO REACH GROUP DECISIONS

By Lambert Jackson Case

The Bethany Press
St. Louis, Mo.

Copyright © 1958

by

THE BETHANY PRESS

Case, Lambert Jackson

How to reach group decisions.   St. Louis, Bethany Press
[1958]

64 p.   22 cm.

1. Decision-making.   2. Forums (Discussion and debate)   3. Meetings.   i. Title.

PN4181.C3   374.24   58—12744 ‡

Library of Congress

Printed in the United States of America

CONTENTS

Chapter One

BARRIERS TO GROUP DECISIONS

Studying the reasons for lack of accomplishment often provides the key to success. It also serves as a warning of what not to do and calls attention to barriers that may prevent a group decision. If these barriers are spotted early in a meeting, they can be sidetracked and eventually eliminated.

THE "RUT" ATTITUDE

One of the first barriers to reaching group decisions is one that has held many groups back—retarded them from achievement, from reaching their goals. It is the "RUT" attitude, which unfortunately is found in many groups today. The members of these groups do not want to make decisions because the decision will involve change, and change usually results in an expenditure of time and effort on the part of someone, and that "someone" may be the person who is faced with the decision. It is much easier to go along in the same old way, even though members of the group are not satisfied and know that a change is needed.

People and groups often fall into this rut. They remember some former experience, which resulted from a decision and remember the time and work involved. Sometimes they overlook all of the good that was accomplished by the decision, just because the change meant responsibility and effort. As a rule the work falls on the shoulders of the same people—year in and year out. This is especially true in a religious group. Thus people know that if a decision is to be made, one which involves a change, the chances are that some of the responsibility will fall on their shoulders and they just sit back and help the group stay in the rut, help to dig it deeper.

One should remember that the main difference between a "rut" and a "grave" is that the latter is deeper and closed at both ends. A group that fails to make decisions is apt to stay in a rut and end up in a grave.

Afraid of Making Mistakes

A second reason for failure to secure decisions is that the group as a whole, or a majority of its members, is afraid of making the wrong decision. They are afraid then that the situation will be worse than it was before.

A lot of people like to be "fence straddlers." If they truly analyzed their thinking and actions, they would see that they have made a decision. They have decided not to decide.

Sometimes making a mistake is the only way to learn which way is wrong and which is right. Experiments are being made today in all phases of life—in our scientific laboratories, in industry, in our social life—to discover the right way. Often these experiments show the wrong results, and the group has to keep right on experimenting until the right formula or method is discovered. If it were not for this experimentation there would be no progress. And, strangely enough, what has been thought to be a mistake, at times, has proved to be a beneficial discovery.

People who won't make decisions because they are afraid that they will make the wrong one, are in just as deep a rut as those who are afraid of the work involved.

One of the best ways to avoid this second problem, of course, is to make as thorough a study of the issue as possible, in advance, so that an intelligent, far-sighted decision can be made. There is always the possibility of error in judgment, but there is not as great a chance, if as much as possible is known about all of the ramifications of the issue involved.

Misunderstandings

Many groups make wrong decisions because they do not understand the problem involved. People do not, as a rule, like to decide something which they do not understand.

If the facts are organized before the meeting, and are explained in clear, specific, precise terms, everyone will know what is involved in the discussion—all of the benefits and all of the problems. The more important the issue is, the more time and effort should be spent in gathering all of the information which relates to it. Then the facts can be studied and an intelligent decision can be made.

Selfish Motives

A fourth difficulty in securing group decisions is that every group is composed of people, and people have a habit of being selfish at times. This old law of self-preservation creeps out every once in awhile.

The members go to a meeting, not with the idea of thinking: "What can I give?" but with the attitude: "What can I get?" Unfortunately, too many are thinking: "What is there in it for me?"

When such an attitude is changed, decisions will be made more quickly, and more wisely.

This should certainly be expected from members of religious groups.

Poor Organization

Finally, many groups fail to make decisions, or find it difficult to make decisions, because they are poorly organized. Sometimes the people who are mainly involved with the issue, those who have the best information, are not present at the meeting. It may be that the group has not the authority to make the decision in question.

Often, decisions are not made or are made with great difficulty, because the meeting is not efficiently directed and controlled by the chairman. Time is wasted on nonessential details; discussion goes off "on tangents"; interruptions are allowed to distract attention.

To hold a meeting where an important decision is to be made should involve very careful planning. Then it should be wisely and efficiently directed by an experienced chairman. He must be able to tactfully guide the discussion and control the actions of the group so that decisions are made which will be constructive and satisfactory to the group.

SUMMARY

Profit by what we have discussed so far.

As a group—or as a member of a group:

1. Be willing to change—decide on issues, even though it will involve time and effort on your part.

2. Have the courage to decide, even though you may make a mistake. Secure all possible information in advance. If you make the wrong decision, correct it by changing and making the right one.

3. Explain the issue at hand so that everyone will understand it. GET THE FACTS.

4. Attend the meeting in an altruistic attitude. Decide on what is best for the group as a whole, no matter how it affects your personal interests.

5. Give careful attention to the organization of the meeting. Select a chairman who will get things done.

TEST

CHAPTER 1

Note: After you have answered the following questions either "Yes" or "No," turn this sheet upside down to check your answers. **Do not check them before you answer the questions.**

	YES	NO
1. Do some of the persons in your group seem to dominate the meetings?	------	------
2. Do some of them waste time on unrelated subjects?	------	------
3. Do you usually have all of the FACTS necessary?	------	------
4. Are the issues to be discussed rather vague?	------	------
5. Are the issues questionable—not understood?	------	------
6. Are the issues explained clearly?	------	------
7. Are they explained so that responsibilities are definite?	------	------
8. Are all of the possibilities of action explored?	------	------
9. Do members allow personal interests to influence them?	------	------
10. Are they afraid of making wrong decisions?	------	------
11. Do they hesitate for fear of responsibility?	------	------
12. Are decisions usually postponed indefinitely?	------	------
13. Are they postponed to a later meeting?	------	------
14. Do you leave meetings feeling that little was accomplished?	------	------

ANSWERS

Questions 3, 6, 7 and 8 should be answered "Yes." All others should be answered "No." If question #13 is answered "Yes," it does not show as much indecision as a "Yes" for question #12.

If you can answer 10 or more correctly, it would indicate that your group is the type that usually makes decisions. Otherwise it needs help. If more than 7 are answered incorrectly, it indicates that some immediate work should be done to educate your group to becoming more decisive.

Chapter Two

HOW TO ARRIVE AT GROUP DECISIONS

Factors Involved

Perhaps the most important and most effective of group decisions are those made by juries. The twelve men or women who sit on a jury often have momentous decisions to make. In a civil case, thousands of dollars can be involved. In a criminal case, the freedom or life of an individual may be at stake. The jury listens to the arguments as presented by the defense and the prosecuting attorneys. Then, after instructions from the judge, the jury adjourns to a private room, where its members discuss the pros and cons of the case, until they arrive at a decision.

Sometimes the decision can be reached in a short time, perhaps a matter of minutes or hours. But, in other cases, especially when the situation is complicated—where either large sums of money are involved, or a human life is at stake—the jury may be out for several days. In the latter instance the twelve members are not allowed to have any contact with the public, once the case has been left in their hands, until they have reached a decision and delivered their verdict.

Ordinarily, the decisions which your group has to make are not as momentous as those of a jury, but to the persons directly involved they are very important. To a great extent, the time and effort involved in making the decision should be determined by its relative importance. This is not always easy to determine. What might appear to be a trivial matter to one person could be considered important to someone else.

Therefore, the matter should be carefully studied to see how many persons it will affect, how much money and/or time are involved, how far-reaching the decision will be, and other factors concerning its importance.

The relative importance of the decision will, or should have, a great deal to do with the amount of information which should be gathered ahead of time, the number of persons who should have a part in discussing and making the decision, and how much time should be spent in arriving at a decision. For example, a committee which meets to plan a Christmas party for the Sunday school, as important as that may seem at the time, will not have as momentous a decision to make as the religious education committee when developing the curriculum for the coming year. A house committee, meeting to decide on what color paint to use in the basement hallway, does not have as important decisions to make as those made by the building committee, when the members are trying to decide whether two hundred or three hundred thousand dollars should be raised to finance the construction of the new educational building.

Types of Decisions

Decisions which a group is called upon to make are of various types.

1. There are the clear-cut "yes" or "no" decisions: Should or should not the choir wear robes? Should or should not Miss Jones be asked to teach the Primary Class? Should or should not the janitor be discharged, and a new man be hired?

Often it is difficult to make a definite "yes" or "no" decision. It appears to be so FINAL. Therefore it may be wise to study the various facts to see if a definite "yes" or "no" has to be given.

It may be possible to attach provisions to the affirmative or negative answer, such as: giving the janitor notice that unless he does a more acceptable job in the future, he will be discharged or deciding to try out Miss Jones as a teacher until she has proved herself an effective teacher with primary children.

13

There are times, however, when a "yes" or "no" decision is necessary. It may be that a decision has been put off because some members seemed undecided about the matter involved. When such decisions have to be made, all of the facts should be carefully studied before the decision is called for. The chairman must be certain that everyone thoroughly understands the issue, and knows what the results will be, depending on the results of the vote. Why it is necessary to take a definite "yes" or "no" vote must be explained so that everyone will know he must make a decision.

When the vote is taken, all votes must be carefully counted especially if the margin is close, so that everyone will feel that the decision was definitely approved or disapproved. Then the final result must be announced so that everyone concerned will know about it.

2. Financial decisions are very important to most groups, and some people dislike being involved in them. But someone has to accept the responsibility or the business of the organization can't progress.

Financial decisions usually are divided into two groups: those involved with "income" and those involved with "expense." Money has to be raised by subscription, by offerings, by drives, by special projects, etc. It is spent through appropriations for salaries, overhead, supplies, music, flowers, and so forth.

As a rule, a board or an executive committee has most to say about the financial matters of an organization, and all important financial decisions must be made by such members. Other groups, or the general membership, may make recommendations or suggestions, but the final decisions usually rest in the hands of the board.

However, even financial decisions differ in importance. Often it is the relative amount of money that makes the difference, or the time involved, or the number of people concerned.

In financial matters involving income, many decisions have to be made—for example:

a. How much money is needed?
b. How soon is it needed?
c. From what sources can it be expected?
d. What methods will be used in securing it?

Decisions involving the spending of money are based on such questions as:

a. How much money shall be, or can be, spent?
b. How is it to be allocated?
c. When should it be spent?
d. Who shall supervise the spending?

It is very important that persons acting as committees and boards, who have the responsibility of either raising or disbursing money, be farsighted, business-minded, practical people. There are important positions and responsibilities for those who are visionary, idealistic and even impractical in most organizations, but they belong on such committees as: program, music, teaching, etc. They should not be charged with the responsibility of making decisions involving financial matters.

3. Another category of decisions might be classified under the general title of ways and means. The term fairly well describes the issues involved. Often a budget or a financial committee will decide how much money shall be raised to cover the budget of an organization, and then turn the matter of actually raising the amount to the "Ways and Means" committee.

People with ideas, those with creative imagination, with the ability to envision many methods and techniques whereby the money can be raised belong in this group.

Such groups handle many other matters, as well, for example, How can a program be carried out? How can membership be increased? How can better attendance be secured and greater participation in activities be encouraged?

4. Another category of decisions concerns problems. Some problems can be very simply decided by a "yes" or "no" vote; others are much more complicated and need special attention.

How Decisions Are Made

Leaders of groups and the groups themselves have influenced —and do influence—the making of decisions.

First, there is the strong-arm method of getting a decision. Unfortunately, some leaders, and some groups, use this method at times. The leader may be so sure of himself, of his knowledge of the issue involved and of how it must be decided, that he uses every means to force the decision of the group, and influences the members to decide his way.

Many members of a committee, or an organization, are not strong minded and are easily swayed by the opinions of others. They will not permit their own opinions—if they have any—to influence them in making a decision contrary to the wishes of other, stronger members of the group.

If a leader or certain members of a group are influential members of the organization or the community, there is often a tendency for other members of the group to go along with their thinking and their decisions rather than expressing their own.

This can be overcome by the leader, or a member of the group, by emphasizing the fact that everyone should express his honest attitude on the issue, and make his own decision, regardless of the ideas of other members.

Second, many group decisions are faulty and not carefully thought out because the discussions on the matter have taken up so much time or ideas, unrelated to the issue at hand, are interpolated. As a result, members of the group make hasty decisions, just to close the discussion, in order to go home to their own personal responsibilities. Much of the fault of such mishandling lies with the way the chairman conducts the meeting and will be discussed more fully in a later chapter.

No matter how long and dragged out the session may be, decisions should not be made as an expediency to bring the discussion to a hurried close. Occasionally a group can make an intelligent decision under such circumstances, but more often the decisions are not carefully made and afterward, the members of the group may regret their choice.

Third, decisions may be made before members of the group have thoroughly investigated the matter. Their thinking is confused. They make a decision and then afterwards question it. Often, the wrong emotions are aroused and when this happens, the issue is clouded. This can be avoided, naturally, if all of the facts have been presented clearly, and if the members do not vote until they thoroughly understand what they are deciding. If a member is confused in his thinking, he should say so, and the matter involved should be explained until he and everyone else do understand it.

Some people do not grasp ideas as quickly as others. Often leaders, who may have a thorough knowledge of the issue, just take for granted that everyone else is just as well acquainted with it as they are, and press for decisions. But, if people feel pressed, and are rushed into decisions before they fully understand the issue, they may fail to accept the responsibility of consummating the project.

Fourth, some leaders and members of groups, gain decisions through the use of flattery, cajolery, and just plain bribery. This is a dishonest method (no matter how it may look on the surface), and certainly should not be approved by any group—especially a religious group. Sometimes it is very cleverly done, and members of the group do not realize that they are being won over and sold on something which they would not honestly approve if they realized what was taking place. Occasionally even religious leaders are so anxious to put over some cherished scheme that they will use such methods to secure group decisions.

Fifth, some decisions are arrived at by compromises. Sometimes they are good, and sometimes they are bad. If there appears to be no meeting of the minds of members of a group and there seems to be a stalemate, then often a compromise is the only decision. Members of each side give up some of their ideas and are willing to accept those of the other side, in order to secure a decision. Such a compromise can be—as we have said—good.

On the other hand, some compromises are not good. They may be worse than no decisions at all. Both sides may leave the meeting in an unenthusiastic frame of mind and feel that little was gained by the decision. Even though they support the decision, they may not support it enthusiastically.

In making a compromise, the opposing groups must be careful that they do not adopt suggestions that will neutralize the constructive effects they had in mind. The compromise should be a step in the right direction. Often it can be, and eventually the full value of the original ideas can be put into practice.

TEST

CHAPTER 2

Note: After you have answered the following questions, turn this sheet upside down to check your answers. **Do not check them before you answer the questions.**

	TRUE	FALSE
1. A matter involving a definite "yes" or "no" does not have to be studied carefully.	------	------
2. It is possible to attach provisions to the affirmative or negative answer.	------	------
3. All voting can be accomplished by asking for a verbal reply.	------	------
4. Financial decisions do not need special attention.	------	------
5. As a rule, important financial decisions are made by a board or executive committee.	------	------
6. Persons making financial decisions should be visionary.	------	------
7. The Ways and Means Committee usually determines the amount of money to be raised.	------	------
8. A leader of a group should not use "strong-armed" methods to secure a decision.	------	------
9. It is all right for a group to make hasty decisions as a matter of expediency.	------	------
10. Some people do not grasp ideas as quickly as do others.	------	------
11. It is good to gain decisions by means of flattery and cajolery.	------	------
12. All compromises are good.	------	------

ANSWERS

Answers to questions 2, 5, 8, and 10 should be answered "True." All of the others should be answered "False." A score of 9 or more is good; 6 or more correct is fair. If you scored 5 or less, you had better study the chapter again.

Chapter Three

MEETING PROCEDURE

Naturally, the procedure of the meeting depends on many factors—the purpose of it, whether or not it is a regular, scheduled meeting of an organization or a special, called meeting, and the business involved.

All meetings should be conducted in an organized, businesslike manner. If a meeting is called for a specific purpose, all plans should be made well in advance so that it is well organized. The chairman should call it to order, appoint a secretary (if one has not been appointed) to cover the minutes or report which will have to be made later. Reports on the business, or issue to be discussed, should be made and discussion directed until every one concerned feels well posted on the information before a decision or vote is called for. If another meeting is necessary, the date and time should be set before adjournment.

If the meeting is a regular, scheduled meeting, it should follow accepted procedure, which usually is as follows:

1. Call to order by presiding officer.
2. Reading of minutes of last meeting by recording secretary, and approval of them.
3. Reading of correspondence by corresponding secretary.
4. Report of officers and approval of group.
5. Reports of standing committees and approval.
6. Reports of special committees and approval.

7. Old business.

8. New business.

9. Adjournment.

Mechanics of the Meeting

Details involved in a well-conducted meeting are familiar to most people but a review will serve as a check list for future meetings.

The Meeting Place

The location of the meeting place, the size of the room and the equipment necessary will depend on the nature of the meeting, the purpose or goal, the number of persons involved, the length of the meetings or meeting, and other factors.

As a rule, it is best to hold the meeting in the customary place, such as the parish house, the educational building, or headquarters of the group. The persons involved know its location and are accustomed to going there. Also, they associate all matters concerned with the organization with the location and most information that may be needed will be available there.

If a room in your church or headquarters is to be used, its size and equipment should be checked ahead of time to be certain all of the necessary facilities are ready. It should be reserved well in advance as such rooms are often in demand.

Several things should be checked when the meeting place is not the usual one:

1. Is the location accessible to all persons involved? If some of the members do not have automobiles, is there a nearby car or bus line? If not, be certain that all have rides with others.

2. Is the room adequate, large enough, but not too large? Does it have enough chairs or seats for the group? If the meeting is to last over a period of time, there must be adequate seating, and comfortable seats.

3. Are the light and ventilation adequate? Heat is important in the winter and air conditioning in the summer. Body comfort can be extremely important, especially if the meeting lasts long. If people are not comfortable, they are apt to get irritable. They may grow restless and not do their best thinking. If they are too uncomfortable, they may rush the decisions and close the meeting in order to get to more comfortable surroundings.

4. In a large room the acoustic properties should be checked. A loud-speaker system is advisable if the room is spacious and the group is large. If people cannot hear what is said, time is often wasted in repetitions, and the audience may not get a clear understanding of the discussion. If a microphone is used, all important remarks should be made over it so that everyone can hear.

5. A lectern or reading stand is important. This gives the speaker a place to lay his notes so that his talk will be much more effective. In a small group meeting, the members may sit around a table, or those conducting the meeting may use a small table for necessary materials and for a pitcher of water and glass.

6. It is advisable to have a blackboard available if the speaker or anyone participating in the discussion needs one. The use of diagrams or visual aids on a blackboard can be conducive to constructive discussion methods and help in securing decisions.

7. It is wise to provide pads and sharpened pencils for those wishing to take notes.

8. Before the meeting all of the information needed for the discussion should be gathered. If any special authorities need to present reports or recommendations, they should be present at a specified time and assigned a limited amount of time for their part in the program.

TIME OF THE MEETING

The time of the meeting is as important as the location and the physical arrangements. A time should be set which will be convenient for most of the people concerned with it. It should be set far enough in advance to allow the persons involved to make their plans to be present. They should be called just previous to the meeting, in case the information has slipped their mind.

Men, as a rule, have to count on night meetings, or on week ends, when they have free time. Usually luncheon meetings are popular with men, if they can get back to their work promptly. Ordinarily, men are more apt to attend meetings if food is also involved, so dinner meetings are quite attractive to them.

Women, on the other hand, usually prefer daytime meetings, especially if they are unescorted. Career women will prefer evening or week-end dates.

Meetings should start promptly and end at a specified time, if possible. Some people are habitually late, but as a rule it is best not to wait for them. If they find that the meetings start on time, they will learn to be on time, especially if they miss some important discussion through being late a time or two.

TEST

CHAPTER 3

Note: After you have answered the following questions, turn this sheet upside down to check your answers. **Do not check them before you answer the questions.**

	TRUE	FALSE
1. Planning is unimportant in getting ready for a business meeting.	------	------
2. Business meetings should follow an accepted procedure.	------	------
3. The size of the room and equipment necessary depend on the nature of the meeting, the purpose of it, the number of persons involved, and how long it will last.	------	------
4. As a rule it is best to meet in your customary place of meeting.	------	------
5. Proper light and ventilation of a room are unimportant.	------	------
6. If a room is small, a loud-speaking system is recommended.	------	------
7. Before the meeting, gather all necessary information.	------	------
8. Blackboards are often helpful.	------	------
9. If you wish to use a room in your headquarters, reserve it well in advance.	------	------
10. Housewives, as a rule, prefer evening meetings.	------	------

ANSWERS

1, 5, 6, and 10 are False and the others True. If, out of your experience, you have scored 7 or more correctly, you have been planning and directing meetings properly. If you score 5 or more correctly you have had fair success. If your score is less than 5, you need to study this chapter more thoroughly and use better methods.

Chapter Four

BUSINESS MEETINGS

In this chapter the techniques which are correct and conducive toward the securing of decisions in a business session will be discussed.

Robert's *Rules of Order* is the accepted book of standard parliamentary procedure and is followed by most organizations. The chairman should know the correct methods which have been proved best and accepted by most organizations for business and discussion meetings. If these methods are used, then no member can say afterwards that the meeting wasn't conducted properly. This will eliminate most dissatisfaction.

Some organizations have one member, who has been authorized to act as parlimentarian, pass on all disagreements as to whether or not correct procedure is being used. He should be an authority on this subject and his word should be accepted. This person should also have studied the constitution and bylaws of the organization and his decisions should be accepted as authority on matters pertaining to this.

If an organization does not have a parliamentarian, the president or chairman should act in this capacity. He, too, must be well versed in correct procedure.

CONSTITUTION AND BYLAWS

Every organization should have a constitution and bylaws. It can be drawn up by a committee and patterned after the constitutions and bylaws of other organizations, and adjusted to suit special needs. In an organization which is part of a larger group, the constitution and bylaws of this group should be studied to be certain none of the new laws will conflict with the policies of the parent group. All members should be present at the meeting at which the constitution is adopted.

Consult Robert's *Rules of Order* for the accepted method to be used in adopting the constitution and bylaws. Then have this document available for reference at all meetings so that no decisions will be made which might conflict with it.

ADOPTION OF REPORTS

The first item of business at most meetings is the reading and acceptance of reports. Often suggestions made in these reports will be the basis for old or new business, where decisions have to be made.

As a rule, the minutes of the last meeting are read by the recording secretary first and should be read so that every one can hear and understand the contents. (This is true of all reports.)

After the report is read, the chairman usually asks if there are any corrections or additions to the report. If someone remembers an item that was omitted, which was important enough to be included, this should be noted and added to the minutes. If an error was made and acknowledged by the secretary or group, the minutes should be corrected.

When this has been done, the chairman should state that if there are no further additions or corrections, the minutes will stand approved as read. This is the accepted plan, although some organizations require a motion to accept the minutes, as well as other reports.

The report of the corresponding secretary usually follows. All correspondence received since the last meeting should be read, and important items noted, to be taken up under old or new business. In some organizations this report may be adopted by acclamation, the same as the minutes. In others a motion to accept is required. When there is no corresponding secretary, the recording secretary serves in this capacity.

Next comes the treasurer's report. If it is complicated, copies of it should be made and passed around to members, to be studied as the report is read. After the reading of the report, a motion to accept or pass on the report is in order. If a member doesn't make this quickly, the chairman may ask: "Will someone move that the treasurer's report be accepted?" or "What is your pleasure with this report?"

The motion should be made, followed by a second. Then the chairman should ask if there is any discussion. If there is none, he puts the motion before the group by stating "All those in favor will say 'Aye,'" and wait for the response. Then he will ask for the "Nays." If there is any question, the vote may need to be counted by a show of hands, and the members for and against noted. If a majority are in favor, he states "The motion is passed and the report is accepted." If it is not passed, further discussion may be necessary and action taken.

The above procedure is followed with all officers' and committee chairmen's reports. Reports of standard (permanent) committees take precedence over those of temporary or special committees. The chairman of a committee may move that the report be accepted to save time.

The passing of the report does not necessarily mean that important issues in it are accepted. It simply means that the findings of the committee—the work accomplished—has been approved. Any important recommendations of the officer or committee may have to be taken up under old or new business, depending under which classification it falls.

OLD BUSINESS

After the reports have been read and accepted, the group is ready for old business. Any matters carried over from a former meeting, or meetings, upon which decisions have not been made, should be taken up by the group. Some of the matters will be suggested by the minutes and others from the reports. As these items are reported, it might be well for the chairman to note them, so that they can be discussed and voted on later.

The issues should be presented to the group one at a time, usually in the order in which they have been brought before the group. However, the group may decide to change the order and take up some very important issue first.

The facts about the issue should be fully explained and all questions answered. But before too much discussion has taken place, the matter should be officially placed on the docket by someone moving for action. A motion must be made and must receive a second, before the issue can be officially discussed or any action taken on it.

In order to bring action and secure a decision on an issue it is sometimes necessary for a chairman to ask for someone to make a motion. There is often a tendency for members of a group to sit back and wait for someone to take the lead, and the chairman can spark action by asking for a motion and for a second.

After the motion has been duly made and seconded it is officially placed before the group for discussion and action. If no one seconds the motion it is automatically lost, for "want of a second," and the chairman should so state.

When the chairman feels that adequate discussion has been held on a matter, he can speed up action by asking:

"Are you ready for the question?"

Someone will usually call for the question, and then the voting on the motion takes precedence over any further discussion.

The chairman should be certain that all members understand the motion, on which they are voting, before calling for the vote. Often it is wise to ask the secretary to restate the motion to avoid confusion on the vote so that no one can say he didn't know what the motion was on which he was voting.

If there is *any* question about the number of "ayes" and "nays" in a vote, always ask for a show of hands, or a ballot vote, to secure an accurate count.

After the motion has been carried the chairman *must* state: "The motion has been carried" (or lost) *before* it is official.

To get things done the chairman should see to it that the members of a group stick to business. This is not an easy job as it is always easy to step on the toes of some sensitive soul whose feelings are hurt easily. But, if the chairman doesn't maintain order and follow strict parliamentary procedure, time will pass by and the business of the meeting will be left undone.

If emotions are aroused during a session and people begin to get personal and say things which stir up animosities, it is up to the chairman to control the situation. This takes a great deal of tact and real leadership, so that the members of the group won't feel he is trying to dominate too much.

On the other hand, "steam-roller" tactics, where the chairman or some dominant member uses pressure of one form or another to get things done, should not be condoned. There should always be adequate time for discussion—especially of important issues—but this discussion must be guided and controlled by the chairman, if progress is to be made.

NEW BUSINESS

New business refers to matters which have not previously come to the attention of the group. They may be the outgrowth of some old business or they may be instigated by some correspondence read by the secretary.

New business may be presented by a committee chairman, as the result of discussions held by the committee or it may be presented by a member. Often new business is referred to a committee, or a member, for further investigation before it is presented for final approval. On the other hand, if all the facts are known and time of performance is imminent, the group may vote on it immediately. If the matter is referred to a committee for further study, it is well to suggest a date when the matter should be reported back for action.

TEST

CHAPTER 4

Note: After you have answered the following questions, turn this sheet upside down to check your answers. **Do not check them before you answer the question.**

	TRUE	FALSE
1. Every organization should have a copy of Robert's *Rules of Order* to check parliamentary procedure.	------	------
2. The chairman adopts the constitution and bylaws for the organization.	------	------
3. Committee reports are the first order of business in all business meetings.	------	------
4. When a committee's report is accepted, all items in it are *automatically* approved.	------	------
5. A motion must be seconded before it can officially discussed.	------	------
6. The treasurer's report can be accepted without a vote to approve it.	------	------
7. An oral vote is the best way to secure an *accurate* decision.	------	------
8. There should always be time for a discussion on a motion before it is voted on.	------	------

ANSWERS

Questions 1, 5, and 8 are True and all others False. If you have not checked them correctly, reread the chapter for the right answers.

Chapter Five

THE DISCUSSION MEETING

As a rule, before a decision can be secured on an issue, a project, or a problem, a discussion is involved. If the subject matter is relatively unimportant, or if there is a general agreement of minds, the discussion may be of short duration. A decision may be reached quickly and it will not be necessary to have an organized and directed discussion session.

However, if there appear to be contrary opinions on the subject matter, and especially if the issue or project is an important one involving a major change of policy, an expenditure of a large sum of money, or the development of an important project, it is well to prepare carefully for and hold one or more discussion sessions. How long they will be and how many are necessary depend on the importance of the subject matter and how contrary are the opinions.

Unfortunately the length and number of meetings do not always depend on the degree of importance of the subject matter to be discussed. Sometimes a relatively unimportant matter can stimulate a great deal of fruitless discussion. This is unfortunate as many people who value their time highly grow disturbed with such needless discussions and often lose interest in organizations because of them. Then, when some important issue is at stake, and these persons are called on for advice and help, they may refuse to serve, remembering their former experience. Therefore it is wise for the chairman to limit the time at the beginning of a discussion.

31

If possible, determine ahead of time how many meetings and how much time will be necessary to discuss the issue or project adequately. This can not always be determined, for unexpected emergencies arise which change the plans. But, if this can be determined, more adequate plans can be made and the people involved can be informed about the time which will be spent. This is especially important if the discussion will involve several meetings.

TYPES OF DISCUSSIONS

There are many different types of discussion meetings. Each has its purpose and each must be planned and executed in a different way.

First, there is the more or less spontaneous discussion that arises where a group is considering a change or is considering ways and means of doing something or is trying to decide which way to move in accomplishing its purpose. Most of the time these discussions should be of short duration and merely have to be controlled and guided by the chairman.

Second, there are the discussions which are planned and executed to give a group information and allow an opportunity for discussion on the subject before a decision is to be made. Usually these are of longer duration and have to be planned and organized ahead of time.

Third, the program type of discussion has no other objective than to give the group an opportunity to hear a subject discussed and to allow participation in the discussion. This is called a round-table discussion.

Fourth, there is the brain-storming type of discussion, which is planned and organized to stimulate creative thinking.

Fifth, many discussion meetings are built around a panel, where a small group opens the discussion with talks and later the members are invited to ask questions. In this case, the members of the panel should present various phases of the subject and represent different points of view. Each member of the panel should be selected because of his knowledge and viewpoint so that the various phases of the subject are adequately covered. The chairman—or moderator—should be neutral and should not express an opinion, but should control and direct both the panel talks and the participation of the audience. Each member of the panel should be allotted a definite time and should be limited to this. He may be given additional time later as a rebuttal or to give explanation that has been necessitated by points of view expressed by other panel members.

When the panel members have given their talks and the meeting has been turned over to general discussion by the audience, questions may be directed to the chair and the answers volunteered by members of the panel, or they may be directed to definite panel members.

Sixth, another type of discussion meeting is the forum. In this instance a talk is usually given by one person and afterwards the audience participates by asking questions of the speaker. In the forum meeting there is usually a chairman who presides, and who directs the discussion period—directing the questions to the speaker for reply. If a large crowd is present, the chairman should repeat the question asked by a member, especially if there is any possibility that it has not been heard by all present. In the discussion or question period the chairman, and not the speaker, is in charge. He should close the meeting at the time scheduled or when he senses that all questions have been answered. Never allow a discussion period to drag.

If there is a feeling that members of an audience will hesitate to participate in such a meeting, it is well to have questions "planted" in advance. Certain members are given questions which may invoke other questions. Often when a speaker has closed his talk, there is a short lull. Members of the audience hesitate in being the first one to ask a question. Once the questions start, others are stimulated, and planted questions will save this uncomfortable lull.

When the group is large, many people who might ordinarily ask questions hesitate in doing so. If this is the case, ask the members of the audience to write out their questions and give them to ushers, who in turn will bring them to the chairman.

In any type meeting careful planning and organization is necessary.

There are many things which make for poor discussion meetings.

First, the issue, project, or subject matter should be made clear at the beginning of the meeting. The topic should be carefully and clearly explained so that everyone concerned will understand it. Many fruitless discussions are held and much time is wasted because people do not know the significance of the subject, or do not understand it.

In a debate, forum, or a planned discussion meeting the session will get off to a good start if *all terms are defined.* After the opening explanatory statement has been made, it might be well for the chairman to ask if there are any questions about it.

All *facts* should be presented by an individual or a committee who has made an advance study of it so that they are made entirely clear to the group. Generalities are not explicit enough. The opening explanation should be long enough to cover all of the facts adequately, but not so long that the group will lose interest in details.

Second, everyone should be given an opportunity to express himself at the meeting. As a rule this can be controlled and guided by the chairman. The chairman might state at the beginning of the meeting that everyone will have an opportunity to express his ideas on the subject. Unless the more timid members of the group are encouraged to speak, some of the more dominant members will monopolize the discussion. Some groups make a rule at the beginning of the meeting that no one may speak on the subject a second time until everyone else has had an opportunity to speak once. Then no one can complain afterwards that he didn't have the opportunity to express his opinion.

When irrelevant subjects are introduced, it is up to the chairman to suggest that the members stick to the subject under discussion. This has to be done tactfully to avoid hurt feelings.

If some member is monopolizing time, the chairman will have to suggest tactfully that time must be allowed for others. Many people are so enthusiastic about certain projects and so interested in their side of an issue that they unknowingly speak oftener and longer than they should. Their enthusiasm must not be dampened but, at the same time, they must not be permitted to dominate the discussion.

A chairman has to be a diplomat, and often must use tact and discretion both to control and motivate the meeting.

Third, the chairman should strive to keep the discussion on a high emotional level. Uncontrolled emotions can lead some individuals into saying and doing things they would not say or do if their emotions were under control. This is especially true when the subject is very close to the heart of someone, or a certain part of the group.

Enthusiasm is good and is to be encouraged. It is a positive emotion and as a rule doesn't irritate others. But negative emotions, when members get angry or are resentful, are dangerous.

When a chairman realizes that certain members are allowing their negative emotions to dominate, he will have to be very diplomatic. It might be well for him to state that the whole purpose of the meeting can be defeated if members cannot control their emotions and keep the discussions on a high, mature level. Sometimes when negative emotions are allowed to dominate, members will start personal arguments and begin to speak directly to another member. This should not be permitted. The chairman should request that all questions be directed to the chair. All personal issues should be left out of the discussion. Otherwise the morale of the group will be affected and the object of the meeting will be defeated.

TEST

CHAPTER 5

Note: After you have answered the following questions, turn this sheet upside down to check your answers. **Do not check them before you answer the questions.**

	TRUE	FALSE
1. If there are contrary opinions, adequate time should be allowed for discussion.	------	------
2. The discussion of an unimportant issue can sometimes waste valuable time.	------	------
3. In a panel discussion only one speaker expresses his views.	------	------
4. In a forum meeting the speaker directs the discussion, which follows his speech.	------	------
5. In any type of discussion meeting all terms should be defined.	------	------
6. When members discuss irrelevant matters, the chairman should redirect their attention to the issue under consideration.	------	------
7. Enthusiasm should be encouraged by the chairman.	------	------

ANSWERS 1, 2, 5, 6, and 7 are **True** and the others **False**. Reread the chapter for the correct answers.

Chapter Six

BRAIN-STORMING SESSION

"Brain storming" is the term given to discussions to stimulate creative thinking. There is nothing new about such activities. Groups of people have been meeting ever since the dawn of time to plan projects and to decide on the ways and means of working out the plan. But in recent years there has been a revitalization of the idea, under the title "brain storming."

It was primitive man's creative thinking that helped him survive the rigors of life in his day. The huge animals living in the primeval forest were swifter on foot, more powerful, and certainly more forocious than the puny little bipeds who roamed over the land in search of food and shelter. But man, through his creative imagination, fashioned the spear, the bow and arrow, and finally the lever and the wheel. He harnessed and tamed animal life and used the beast to aid him in his fight for existence. The tribes who had leaders with creative imagination survived and ruled. Those who didn't, were either killed off or became enslaved to those who used creative thinking.

Our pioneer forefathers were required to use creative thinking in order to survive. They left the soft life of their homelands and came over to a new world where they too had to fight for existence. Those who used their imagination to build and furnish their homes, to plant and raise their crops, and to provide the necessities of life built a civilization out of a wilderness. They pushed their way westward—still planning and building—until they settled and developed the entire country.

Modern living hasn't required creative imagination in order for man to survive. He can buy most anything he needs at the corner drugstore or the supermarket. This is especially true in urban life, where he has only to push a button or flip a switch to get things done.

There have always been a few people who dreamed dreams and had the stamina and ability to develop the dreams. They have been the inventors, the research scientists, the artists, the writers and the composers. Science and medicine have been continuously advanced by the creative thinkers. In more recent years industry and business have encouraged creative thinking and today most of the large enterprises have laboratories where men and women spend all of their time in research and experimentation.

There isn't a phase of business or professional life where creative thinking doesn't pay dividends today. Even the housewife has a more productive and happier life if she uses creative thinking to plan and carry out her work.

Both Constructive and Destructive

Today many leaders in the psychological fields have been studying and experimenting with the idea of creative thinking. Out of this activity has come suggestions which seem to stimulate creative thinking and to develop a plan of operation whereby it can be put to practical use. The same technique applies, whether it is used by an individual or a group.

Creative power seems to reside in the subconscious mind. Psychologists agree that everyone is born with ability. Children have tremendous imaginative powers. But, as they grow up, the ability is often thwarted by their elders—in the home, the school, and the church. Instead, it should be encouraged, controlled, and guided.

Imagination, uncontrolled and misdirected, can be very destructive. If the wrong motive stimulates this powerful force, it destroys life. For example, electricity can be used to cook a meal, warm the home, and manufacture products. Or it can kill a criminal in the electric chair. Atomic energy can be used in an atomic bomb or in a power plant. It all depends on the creative thinking behind it—how, why, and where it is used.

But today, both in business and industry, individuals and groups are harnessing their creative thinking for peaceful and constructive purposes. It can be used by individuals and groups, in all walks of life, in all types of organizations, and much good will come of it, if the purpose is constructive.

TECHNIQUES

As a result of the thinking and experimenting of leaders in the creative thinking field, certain steps have been worked out to develop and organize "imagineering" (a term used in industry today). It is not a hard and fast set of rules, but if followed step by step, it seems to be the best method to develop creative thinking and to put it to work.

Alex Osborn and other prominent writers in this field, suggest something like the following plan of operation for both individuals and groups.

First, there must be a purpose, a goal, a problem, or a project. Ideas do not seem to come unless there is stimulation, a need. All participants must be concentrating on the same project or problem which should be clearly defined so that all members understand it and start out with the same goal in mind.

Second, facts must be gathered. Ideas as to how the problem can be solved or the project developed will be suggested by the group. As these ideas are expressed, they must be written down on a large blackboard or large wall charts or on paper or cards.

All of the ideas expressed by anyone in the group must be written down. Some of them, even many of them may be unusable but at this stage of the process all of the ideas, no matter how fantastic, should be noted. None of the ideas should be analyzed or discounted at this point. Once they start to be evaluated, the flow of ideas seems to stop.

Search for ideas should continue as long as they come to mind, even if some of them are duplicates and have already been expressed.

Third, the ideas should be organized into various categories, culling out the duplicates. At this stage, the ideas still should not be analyzed or evaluated. They should simply be grouped according to ways in which they will be put into effect, or into which department they will fall, or whose responsibility they will be in the development process.

Fourth, after the ideas have been organized the members, collectively or in smaller groups, may begin to think of alternatives to each idea that has already been expressed. Each person should ask himself:

What other alternatives are there to this idea?

    a. If it was revised, what idea would it give?

    b. Should it be bigger—smaller—faster—slower—upside down?

    c. What can I add to it or detract from it?

    d. What contrasting ideas can I get? Suppose I used the opposite idea—what would happen?

    e. What similar ideas can I imagine?

By doing this, each idea will suggest others and eventually the original group of suggestions will have been doubled or tripled.

Fifth, there is the incubation, or simmering period. Even this is not the analyzing or evaluating stage. The individual, or group of individuals, is just allowing the ideas to simmer in their minds. Even in this stage, other ideas will appear and should be noted. This period may be short or quite long, depending on the number of suggested ideas.

Sixth, finally the period of the analysis or synthesis is reached. Now the ideas can be analyzed and evaluated. Reason, judgment, and past experience can come into the picture. Discussion includes such questions as: Will this work? Which idea will work best? Which will have immediate results? Which will be best in the long run? Which will cost less? Which will be the most efficient? Which will be the most practical? Which can be used by our members, and would not require outside help?

This will result in weeding out the ideas that are unusable or at least not the best.

Seventh, the ideas which seem feasible or probable should be tested. If they don't work, they should be discarded or changed. The group should stick with this process until it has found those ideas which will work, or until it knows that none of them will work.

If none of the ideas will work, the process will have to be repeated with a whole new set of ideas.

Creative thinking requires stamina—sticking with the process until a workable solution to the problem or ideas is reached.

TEST

CHAPTER 6

Note: After you have answered the following questions, turn this sheet upside down to check your answers. **Do not check them before you answer the questions.**

	TRUE	FALSE
1. Brain-storming sessions stir up creative thinking.	------	------
2. Modern living stimulates creative thinking.	------	------
3. Science and medicine have been advanced by creative thinking.	------	------
4. The first step in creative thinking is to gather ideas.	------	------
5. When gathering ideas, each idea should be analyzed as it is expressed.	------	------
6. The "incubation" period is for the purpose of *proving* the ideas expressed.	------	------
7. Creative thinking often involves stamina.	------	------
8. Experiment with new ideas as quickly as they are suggested.	------	------

ANSWERS

1, 3, and 7 should be checked "True" and all others "False." Reread the chapter for corrections.

Chapter Seven

HOW TO SOLVE PROBLEMS

A problem is something to be solved, whether it is in the field of mathematics or in the field of life's experiences. The fact that it is a problem shows that it has a solution.

If we face a problem in mathematics, physics, or chemistry, we figure out the formula to be used and we work on it until we solve it. But when we, as individuals or as groups, face life problems, we often take different attitudes, many of them very negative. Some people adopt a martyr complex. They feel the world is against them and they must expect bad luck. They say they will just have to accept the problem as "the Lord's will" and "grin and bear" it. Others take a defeated attitude from the very beginning. Immediately they run away from the problem or put off the facing of it. As far as they are concerned, it is insurmountable.

A negative attitude has never solved problems. If a person, or a group, faces a problem, there should only be one attitude: "The problem *can be solved*." From then on it is a matter of working out the best solution.

There are steps in this just the same as there are steps in the solving of a math problem.

First, the problem must be faced and formulated. It should be written out on the blackboard (if it is your organization's problem) or on a piece of paper. Writing it out does two things:

It crystallizes the problem and focuses the attention upon it. While the problem is still in the mind, it may be hazy and quite general. Writing it down separates it from other problems and makes it specific. Then, putting the problem on paper and removing it from the mind objectifies it and separates it from the emotions. Uncontrolled emotions can magnify a problem until they make a "mountain out of a molehill." Fear, anxiety, worry, and pessimism have never solved a problem. They intensify the problem and multiply it until it may seem impossible.

Second, the problem must be analyzed and observed from all angles. Only by doing this can one tell whether or not he has found all the facts.

For example, a man who was an expert department store window trimmer and display man used this method. Often when he was working with the display in the window, he couldn't get the desired effect. So he would go outside— perhaps across the street—and take a look at his display from that distance. It was then that he could see the attractive and unattractive features. Then he would go back into his window and correct the defects.

The same idea can be used by moving away from the problem and taking an over-all, impersonal attitude.

Third, the problem must be evaluated. Many people and groups feel that their problems are much more difficult than those of anyone else. But when the problems of one group are compared with those of another, they take on a different perspective.

44

The problem should raise questions something like these: How important is this problem? How much difference will it make in my life six months or a year from now? If it isn't solved, will it make much difference in the scheme of things? Nine times out of ten, a problem that has been truly evaluated, will become smaller in relationship to others and can be dismissed.

Fourth, if the problem is vital, after this careful evaluation, then steps should be taken to solve it. The emotions should be kept out of the process and the formula which will solve it should be applied.

TEST

CHAPTER 7

Note: After you have answered the following questions, turn this sheet upside down to check your answers. **Do not check them before you answer the questions.**

	TRUE	FALSE
1. Some problems do not have a solution.	------	------
2. If you can't solve a problem, put off the solution.	------	------
3. To crystallize a problem, face it and formulate a solution.	------	------
4. The closer you are to a problem, the easier it is to solve.	------	------
5. *All* problems are important and should be worked on until solved.	------	------

ANSWERS

Only 3 should be "True." If you marked others, you had better reread the chapter. If you have difficulty in solving problems, reread it anyway.

Chapter Eight

THE CHAIRMAN

The chairman plays an important part in group discussions. Sometimes the success or failure of accomplishment rests on his shoulders.

It is sometimes difficult to convince one of a group to assume the responsibilities of chairmanship. As a result, one who is not fitted to lead, assumes the role and little if any progress is made at a meeting.

The more important the purpose of a meeting is, the more care should go into the selection of a chairman. Many times a person is elected or appointed to the position of chairman because of his influence, prestige, or because of some material contribution to an organization. Such a person does not necessarily have leadership qualities, and as a result much time is lost in ineffective talking on or off the subject, wrangling over petty nonessentials, or misdirected discussion.

His Qualifications

It is not often that a person can be found who will have all of the qualities of an ideal chairman, but these qualities can act as a guidepost in the selection of a person who seems to have most of them.

First, he must be dominant, he must have the ability to control and guide the discussions and business of a group. This is one of the basic tests of leadership—to be able to control a situation without creating resentment.

47

For that reason the chairman should be a person of authority, one who naturally commands the respect of others. People should value his opinions and feel he knows what he is talking about and what he is doing. If possible, he should be an authority on the particular subject under discussion. If not, an expert, a consultant who is an authority, should be present at the meeting.

For example, the chairman of a church board, to be an "authority," should be familiar with the working organization and business of the church. A person may be a successful businessman, but may know very little about church organization, policies, procedures, and so forth. He may not be able to transfer his ability to manage a business to the management of church affairs. If he can't, then he would not be a good chairman of a church board.

A chairman of a religious education committee should be familiar with the latest trend in religious education and with the religious education program of his church, and he should know the personnel connected with the department.

Such authority will naturally command the respect of the members of his group and they will follow his leadership.

The chairman's dominance should not be in the form of pressure. He *leads* rather than *pushes* the group into a decision. He gives the members of a group the feeling that they all have a chance to express their opinions adequately, but he controls the discussion so that time is not wasted. This dominance, to be most effective, should be sparked by persuasiveness. A person can be dominant, but not persuasive. In other words, he can control the thinking and actions of the group, but he may not be able to persuade the group to act. The first quality needs to be coupled with this second, to be effective.

In a sense, a successful leader of a group must be a salesman. He must be able to sell (persuade) the group on himself as an authority, and then sell (persuade) the members of the group to think and to act. This does not mean that he should persuade the group to believe that his ideas on an issue are necessarily right. In fact, as a rule, the chairman does not express an opinion on an issue unless it is asked. And even then, his opinion should be weighed carefully, and considered only in relationship to his knowledge of the issue involved.

The qualities of confidence and enthusiasm are helpful to persuasiveness. A group soon senses whether or not a chairman is sincerely interested in a project or problem by the enthusiasm he expresses concerning it.

He must be certain that all issues are clearly understood by all members of the group, before a decision is made. This may take time and often a great deal of explanation before the issue is clear.

He should not "railroad" decisions, but after allowing adequate time for discussion, should *lead* the group into a decision.

Acting as a chairman of a group meeting often involves patience on the part of the leader. He has probably made a more thorough study of the issue involved than the other members. Therefore, he must have the patience to wait and not force a decision until all members are made acquainted with all information needed to intelligently make individual decisions. He must have patience with people who "get off the subject" and take up time on extraneous subjects, and still be able to suppress them tactfully.

A successful chairman should be an optimistic, affirmative, positive thinker. As a rule there are people on a committee or in a group that can think of all the ways why something cannot be done, or why it will not work. The chairman has to be able to show the group that it *can* be done, *if* the group decides on it and everyone will get behind it. If the chairman is negative, or even lukewarm, the members of the group will sense this and not be in favor of making a decision.

He must be able to think clearly, and often he must be able to think quickly. The two are often not synonymous. If the chairman cannot understand the issue involved, he will not be able to guide the group into a clear understanding of it. Therefore he should have the type of mind which grasps ideas quickly and in turn can explain them to the group. Without clear explanations some members are going to vote on decisions with misunderstanding and misgivings and later they may claim they were pressured into making a decision.

Finally, a chairman should have a sense of humor. He need not be a comedian or a clown but he should have enough sense of humor so that discussions and arguments will not upset him. He will be able to steer the group more intelligently by not taking them too seriously. He can smile when others are down-hearted and ready to give up. He does not grow tense and allow the situation to worry him. A chairman's sense of humor is often called on to alleviate tense situations and untangle emotional outbursts.

How the Chairman Is Selected

The chairman may be selected by the methods set forth in the constitution and bylaws of the group. He will be elected by the membership or appointed by a person who holds a position of higher authority. Both of these methods have strong and weak points. Election is considered the most democratic method. But often when a chairman is elected by a group, not very much thinking is involved. On the spur of the moment someone looks over the crowd and names someone who looks as though he might accept the nomination.

Often the most popular person or the one having the most friends present is elected. He may turn out to be a very ineffective leader and have many negative qualities.

On the other hand, if a chairman is appointed by some authority, a group may feel it didn't have a voice in the selection, or that favoritism was involved.

As a rule, and especially if the office of leader is a very important one like the chairman of a board, the chairman of a building committee, or the superintendent of the church school, much time and attention should be given to the selection. Ordinarily this can be best handled by a nominating committee.

Members of such a committee should be persons who will give adequate time and attention to the job. They should be well acquainted with the constituency involved. They should be unbiased and not use influence in favor of some favorite candidate.

They should be appointed far enough in advance of an election to carefully survey the membership and select the best-qualified person for the job. Then they should contact the person to be certain he can and will serve, if elected. To secure the right person often takes time and a great deal of selling.

When the report of the nominating committee is presented, the fact should be stressed that the committee has selected their nominee carefully and a statement should list his qualifications.

As a rule, most organizations still insist on nominations from the floor to protect the democratic plan of action. And unless the qualifications of the nominee are stressed, all of the work of the nominating committee will have been in vain and some unqualified person may be nominated from the floor and elected.

The Job of Chairmanship

A chairman should think of his position as a *trust* on the part of the members of a group. He is responsible to the members who have elected him and should be faithful to that trust.

If he hasn't made a study of the purpose, the policies, and procedures of the group, he should do so at once. As chairman, he should be the best-informed person in the group. At the same time, he should try to maintain an unbiased, neutral opinion on all issues, to be fair and considerate in his ruling.

He should be familiar with the rules that govern the group (usually the constitution and bylaws) and know the rudiments of parliamentary procedure.

As quickly as possible, he should become acquainted with the members of the group, especially as to their abilities, their willingness to serve, and their dependability.

The chairman should be present at all meetings and begin the meeting *on time* unless a member has a bona fide reason for being late and arrangements have been made to wait for him. If members are late the first time or two, because of

51

former practices, they will soon learn that they miss out on important business when they are late, and in the future will come on time.

It is not possible to know all of the business that will transpire at a meeting, therefore time should be allowed for emergencies. But it is wise to learn ahead of time, as far as possible, what business will transpire.

If some matters are more important than others, let this be known to the members so that adequate time can be allowed for their discussion and appraisal. Often, if this is not done, matters of secondary importance take up more time than necessary and the right amount of time is not available when the important issues come up for discussion. The group should not rush through their secondary matters without careful consideration, but the chairman should carefully steer the discussion so that the business of the meeting is handled in proper evaluation as to importance.

Planning of the agenda in advance of the meeting, being certain that all officers and chairmen know their responsibilities and are ready with their reports coupled with the right amount of dominance on the part of the chairman will insure a productive and successful meeting.

TEST

CHAPTER 8

Grade yourself on the qualities a successful chairman should have. Score yourself from 1 to 5, figuring 5 as excellent and 1 as poor. Be honest in scoring yourself. Where you find a quality graded 1 or 2, decide to improve that particular quality.

	5	4	3	2	1
DOMINANCE					
PERSUASIVENESS					
PATIENCE					
OPTIMISM					
LOGIC					
SENSE OF HUMOR					
UNDERSTANDING					
PROMPTNESS					
CAREFUL PLANNING					
DEPENDABILITY					

Chapter Nine

OTHER OFFICERS

THE SECRETARY

In a temporary group, organized only for the purpose of developing a project or solving a problem, the secretary has a short-term responsibility. But even though he will serve for only a short time, his work is very important. If he is to act as secretary of a committee or organization over a long period of time, his responsibilities will be still more important.

A secretary of a temporary committee is often appointed by the chairman, or suggested by the group. Sometimes volunteers for the position are called for, and a person who is willing to do the work will respond. If the time and responsibilities involved are not great, a volunteer may be acceptable.

If the secretary is to serve for a longer term, he is usually elected when the other officers are elected at the time set aside for this. If the committee or organization is a large one, and the secretary will have a great deal of work, the office is often split into two positions: the recording secretary and the corresponding secretary.

The main responsibility of the recording secretary is to record the minutes of the meeting and to read them at succeeding meetings. Minutes should be recorded accurately and legibly. They should be complete—including all business, noting the names of the makers of all motions, the results of the motions, and all important discussions. They should be as brief as possible, not including any extraneous, unimportant matters. The recording secretary should type the minutes if possible. Sometimes, at the request of the organization or committee and particularly if the group is small, he may be asked to send copies of the minutes to the members so that they can study them before the next meeting. Copies of all important reports should be attached to the minutes and kept in permanent form for future reference.

The corresponding secretary is responsible for all correspondence. He receives most of the letters which are sent to the group and, at the direction of the group, answers all correspondence. He should keep the chairman or president informed on all important correspondence as quickly as possible after receiving it. As a rule, he will digest the details of the letters and report on the main substance of them at the meeting (to save time) unless the entire letter is considered important and he is asked to read the letter intact. When there are long intervals between meetings, the corresponding secretary may acknowledge the receipt of the letter to the writer and state that the matter involved will be presented to the group at the next regular meeting. There are times when a special meeting may be necessitated because of emergency matters involved in correspondence. The calling of such a meeting is the responsibility of the chairman or president or the executive committee—if such a committee exists and has been informed about the matter.

The corresponding secretary reads all correspondence, either in part or intact, at each meeting. Then he is directed by the group as to how he should reply. He should be careful to carry out the wishes of the group carefully and in good form. (Books on the subject of correct letter writing are available in most libraries.) Sometimes the chairman or president of a group will insist that copies of all correspondence written by the secretary, be sent to him so that he can be kept informed.

When the secretary of a group both records the minutes and acts as correspondant, he has the dual responsibility as discussed above. It can readily be seen that the position of secretary is a very responsible one. He is the one who maintains the permanent record of the meetings of the group and much may depend on the reliability of his records in years to come. Through his correspondence he is acting as the agent of the group and those with whom he corresponds judge his group by this correspondence. As a rule he should be the type of person who will carry out orders accurately and who likes detail kind of work. If he doesn't use a typewriter, he should write legibly so that his records and letters can be easily read and understood. Typewritten records and letters are advisable, especially when carbon copies are necessary.

The Treasurer

The importance of the office of treasurer depends on the size of the group, the length of time he will serve, and especially the amount of money to be supervised by him.

If the amount of money is quite large, the treasurer should be bonded. But even though the treasury is small, the treasurer should be a very responsible person—one who can be trusted with the funds of the group.

As a rule all funds should be kept in a bank account, all checks should be signed by two persons—usually the chairman or president as well as the treasurer. He sends out checks only as instructed by the group although he may be allowed to pay small accounts (up to a designated amount) as they fall due.

He makes out a report and reads it at each business meeting, listing the previous balance, receipts and expenditures during the period, and the present balance. A copy of this is given to the secretary to be attached to the minutes. Some groups insist that copies of the treasurer's report be given to all members so that they can be studied by members as he reads it.

As a rule, the treasurer makes an annual report at the end of his term of office and his books should be audited. (This is a protection for the treasurer as well as the group.)

The person appointed or elected to this position should understand at least simple bookkeeping procedures and be able to present an intelligent report.

Vice President

The vice president usually acts in a responsible capacity only when the president is unable to do so. Many groups give the vice president added responsibility by making him chairman of a very important committee, such as program, membership, or ways and means.

In large organizations there may be more than one vice president. They should be elected according to the order in which they would serve in the absence of the president (first vice president, second vice president, etc.). These various vice presidents may act as chairmen of several of the important committees.

In some organizations it is customary for the vice president to be the president the succeeding year. If this is true, the person should be selected with this in mind, as he will be training for the executive position during his term as vice president.

Committees

The number and responsibilities of committees differ, according to the size, length of term, and importance of the organization. As a rule, there are two types of committees in an organization: standard and temporary.

The standard committees are permanent and usually serve for a given term. Temporary committees are set up to develop and execute a specified project and are disbanded or dismissed after their responsibilities have been completed.

In a large organization there is usually an executive committee, made up of certain of the officers who are given the authority to meet and carry out routine matters which do not necessitate group action and approval. Also they may meet previous to the regular meetings and organize the business to be presented and discussed by the members. This saves the time of the members and is a good policy, provided—and this is a warning—the executive committee does not use too much authority and make decisions which should rightfully be made by the members of the group.

57

The standard committees which most organizations appoint are: membership, finance, ways and means, program, reception, and house committees. In addition, churches usually add religious education, music education, flower, transportation, visiting, sick, and others.

The name of the committee fairly well defines the nature of its responsibilities which vary with different groups.

In many churches a church council is organized to include the chairmen of the main committees and the heads of the various organizations, such as the superintendent of the church school, the president of the Ladies' Aid, the president of the Men's Club, etc. It has proved to be very helpful and effective in many churches, and anyone interested should study the idea further in books on church organization.

TEST

CHAPTER 9

Note: After you have answered the following questions, turn this sheet upside down to check your answers. **Do not check them before you answer the questions.**

	TRUE	FALSE
1. Almost anyone can act as secretary of an organization.	------	------
2. The recording secretary answers all correspondence, even when there is a corresponding secretary.	------	------
3. The treasurer needs only to report the present bank balance at the regular meetings.	------	------
4. The vice president's position should be considered important and the person who holds it should be chosen wisely.	------	------
5. The secretary need not keep the president or chairman informed on important correspondence.	------	------
6. Standard committees are set up for special events which just take place occasionally.	------	------
7. All organizations need the same committees.	------	------
8. The executive committee should meet between regular organization meetings to consider important issues.	------	------

ANSWERS

4 and 8 should be answered "True" and all the others "False." If you checked some incorrectly, reread the chapter to discover the right answers.

Chapter Ten

THE PARTICIPANTS

In our democratic way of doing things it is the members of the group who are truly the most important part. They make the majority of the decisions through discussing the issues and voting on the motions. They elect the officers who direct the group; also they can ask them to resign if the officers are not carrying out the wishes of the group. In some instances the members relinquish this responsibility and even though they criticize and openly disapprove of the manner in which the business of the organization is being administered by the officers, they do nothing about it. If their opinions are not those of the majority, there may be some reason for no concerted action. But if their disagreement with the administration involves important matters, some type of action should be taken.

In the constitution and bylaws of most organizations, provisions are set up whereby a special meeting may be called, upon the written request of a minimum number of members, for just such action.

One of the first responsibilties of a member of a group is to attend all meetings, except for illness or emergencies. An inactive member is of very little value to any organization. He should be there on time. Being late is often just a bad habit. Naturally there are times when it cannot be avoided. But a truly *active* member of a group will be present at the meeting when it is scheduled to begin its activities.

The member's other big responsibility is to participate. He should keep his ears and eyes open; listen to the reports; ask questions, if certain issues are not clear; take part in the discussion. He should not talk just to be heard, but if he has an opinion, he should express it. These opinions should be based on facts and give additional information, and not just a repetition of some idea already expressed unless a statement of this sort has been requested.

Some people have a habit of not expressing their opinions until the session is over and then do a lot of complaining and criticizing. The time for voicing an opinion is when the matter is being discussed. Once it is voted on and decided, it is well to forget any contrary opinion and co-operate with what the majority decided.

The member must be ready to make motions. Officially, an issue should not be discussed until it has been presented before a group in the form of a motion, and seconded. Often members of a group retard decisions because no one officially moves that the issue be put to a vote. The motion should be stated clearly, specifically, and audibly. Otherwise it may require amendments, which may waste time.

As quickly as a motion is made, someone who favors the discussion on the subject should second it. Again this speeds up discussion. A second of a motion does not necessarily mean approval; it merely opens the discussion. A good member should be ready to vote when the issue is brought to a vote.

One called to serve on a committee or to secure information, should accept the responsibility. He should not accept it, however, unless he expects to carry through with it, for the group will be depending on him for the service. He should be willing to do his part even though it may mean a personal sacrifice.

Participation carried out conscientiously brings great satisfaction. It is a responsibility of membership in any group, and when carried out sincerely and wisely, brings great rewards.

TEST

CHAPTER 10

Check yourself to see if you are participating as you should in your organization's meetings.

	YES	NO
1. I attend only meetings which I feel are important.	------	------
2. I do not participate in the discussion because I do not think my opinions will be considered.	------	------
3. I do not second motions unless I am in favor of them.	------	------
4. I ask questions when my thinking is not clear on the issue.	------	------
5. I vote only on motions which affect me personally.	------	------
6. I want to be on time at meetings but allow other matters to make me late occasionally.	------	------
7. The members of an organization have very little responsibility.	------	------

ANSWERS

Only 4 should be answered "Yes." All others should be answered "No," by the active participant.

Chapter Eleven

HOW TO PUT DECISIONS TO WORK

How can people be motivated to accomplish the task ahead? Naturally each problem or project has its own characteristics and must be dealt with according to its own procedures and responsibilities.

Much depends on the frame of mind the group takes toward the project from the very beginning. If there is any doubt about the possibility of carrying out the project to a successful completion, the project may be doomed from the very beginning.

Therefore, from the start a positive attitude should be adopted. *It can be done.* During the war there was a slogan which read: "The *possible* can be done immediately; the *impossible* may take more time and effort."

As soon as the project has been authorized, the techniques of setting it in motion should be organized. The action may involve only one person. In this case, one who can do it best, who will accept the responsibility, and who will accomplish the task in the given time should be selected.

If the accomplishment of the task involves more than one person, they should be selected just as carefully. A person with leadership ability should be selected to *direct* the carrying out of the task or project. The more important the task, the greater care should be spent in selecting the people who will carry it to completion, and the more important the leadership. If the job will involve a considerable amount of time, this fact should also be taken into account and the persons involved should be so advised. This does not mean that a busy person should not be

63

asked to serve. Often it is the busy people who get things done and who can be depended on to carry through. But members who have not proven their ability should not be overlooked. Willingness to serve is to be commended, but the person volunteering his services must have the *ability* as well as the desire to carry out the task involved.

As a rule, it is well to set dates during which the project is to be accomplished. If expense is necessary, a budget should be planned and the group should be instructed as to how much money has been allowed.

All instructions should be clear and explicit as to just what has been decided about the project. These instructions should be in written form so that there will be no question about them. If some part is not understood, questions should be asked before operation on the project begins.

If the task is complicated, like a financial campaign or a membership drive, much time should be spent in organization. Responsibility should be delegated to many people. This divides the work and makes all members feel they have responsibilities.

Instruct every member who is participating as to what is expected of him and when it is expected. The one in charge should select helpers and then turn the details over to the person or persons involved. He should check up on progress periodically, but should not appear to be nagging or interfering. On the other hand, if he learns that someone is falling down on the job, he should advise him tactfully at first. Then if he continues to fail to live up to responsibility, the task should be given to someone else who can and will do it.

The leader of a group or the member who has been selected to carry out a project should stick with it until it has been completed. Even though he gets discouraged when the going is rough, he must do his best right up to the end. It takes stamina and determination to stick with the ship, especially after some members of the group have given up. But when the job is done and the goal reached, there will be a wonderful feeling of accomplishment and fulfillment.